AGS

Physical Science
Student Workbook

by
Robert Marshall
and
Donald H. Jacobs

AGS®

American Guidance Service, Inc.
Circle Pines, Minnesota 55014-1796
800-328-2560

Printed in the United States of America

ISBN 0-7854-1019-8

Product Number 90292

A 0 9 8 7 6 5 4 3 2

Table of Contents

Compare and Contrast

Directions: When you compare and contrast things or ideas, you tell how they are alike and how they are different. Compare and contrast each pair below.

1. METER—LITER
a. How they are alike

_____

_____

_____

_____

b. How they are different

_____

_____

_____

_____

2. CENTIMETER—MILLIMETER
a. How they are alike

_____

_____

_____

_____

b. How they are different

_____

_____

_____

_____

3. GRAM—METER
a. How they are alike

_____

_____

_____

_____

b. How they are different

_____

_____

_____

_____

4. KILOGRAM—KILOMETER
a. How they are alike

_____

_____

_____

_____

b. How they are different

_____

_____

_____

_____

5. MILLIMETER—MILLIGRAM
a. How they are alike

_____

_____

_____

_____

b. How they are different

_____

_____

_____

_____

Metric Terms Review

Part A

Directions: Match each term in Column A with its meaning in
Column B. Write the correct letter on the line.

Column A   Column B

_____ **1.** gram   **a.** Amount of matter

_____ **2.** mass   **b.** The basic unit of length in the metric system

_____ **3.** liter   **c.** The unit of mass in the metric system

_____ **4.** centimeter   **d.** The unit of length in the metric system equal to
                                       1/1,000 of a meter
_____ **5.** meter
                                  e. The basic unit of liquid volume in the metric system
_____ **6.** millimeter
                                  f. A unit of length in the metric system equal to 1/100 of
_____ **7.** linear   a meter

                                  g. Pertaining to length

Part B

Directions: Unscramble the word or words in parentheses to
complete each sentence below.

8. A _____ is a unit of metric mass equal to 1/100 of a gram.
         (remacting)

9. A _____ is equal to 1,000 grams.
         (magikrol)

10. A _____ is equal to 1,000 meters.
          (trimekole)

11. A _____ is a system of measurements with units based on 10.
          (tecrim metsys)

Systems of Measurement

Directions: The table below describes some unusual units of
measurement. Each unit has a metric equivalent.
Complete the table with the help of a dictionary or other
reference. The first item is done for you as an example.

Uncommon Units of Measurement		
Unit	**Description**	**Equals (Metric)**
1. Knot	Unit used to measure air and wind speed: equals 1 nautical mile per hour	about 2 kilometers per hour
2. Carat	Unit of weight for gemstones	
3. Hand	Unit of length for measuring height of horses	
4. League	Unit of distance in measuring land: 2-1/2 to 4-1/2 miles	
5. Light year	Unit of distance equal to the distance light travels through space in one year	
6. Furlong	Unit of distance in measuring land: 220 yards	
7. Astronomical unit	Unit of distance based on the distance between the earth and the sun	
8. Fathom	Unit of length used to measure the depth of water: 6 feet	
9. Cable	Unit of length used at sea, equal to 100 to 120 fathoms	
10. Pica	Unit of length used in printing: about 1/6 inch	

Math Connection: Metric Measurements

Directions: Complete the indicated calculations, then simplify your
answers.

1.   12 centimeters   5 millimeters
   +   5 centimeters   3 millimeters

2.   10 meters   8 centimeters
   +   9 meters   9 centimeters

3.   22 meters   4 centimeters
   +   3 meters   5 centimeters

4.   20 meters   10 millimeters
   +   23 millimeters

5.   10 centimeters   5 millimeters
   + 22 centimeters   8 millimeters

6.   6 meters   2 centimeters
   +   4 meters

7.   23 millimeters
   +   3 millimeters

8.   11 meters   9 millimeters
   +   8 meters   6 millimeters

9.   39 meters   9 millimeters
   +   1 meter   6 millimeters

10.   20 meters   7 centimeters
   +   5 centimeters

11.   19 meters   8 centimeters
   −   7 meters   5 centimeters

12.   21 meters   12 centimeters
   − 19 meters   10 centimeters

13.   12 meters   2 centimeters
   −   9 meters   9 centimeters

14.   3 meters   7 centimeters
   −   1 meter   8 centimeters

15.   18 meters   2 centimeters
   −   9 centimeters

16.   7 centimeters
   −   4 millimeters

17.   30 meters   4 centimeters
   −   3 meters   7 centimeters

18.   8 meters   7 centimeters
   −   5 meters   7 centimeters

19.   7 centimeters   6 millimeters
   −   8 millimeters

20.   9 meters
   −   6 centimeters

Math Connection: Metric Solutions

Part A

Directions: Perform the indicated operations, then simplify your
answers.

1. 2.4 grams $\times$ 5 = _____

2. 20 grams $\times$ 10 = _____

3. 34.5 grams $-$ 10 grams = _____

4. 13 cm $-$ 5 cm = _____

5. 28 grams $\div$ 7 = _____

6. 30 meters $+$ 15 = _____

7. 39.39 meters $\div$ 13 = _____

8. 8 centimeters $\times$ 7 = _____

9. 7 meters 5 centimeters $\times$ 6 = _____

10. 5 cm 8 mm $\times$ 11 = _____

Part B

Directions: Calculate these areas. Include the correct units.

11. 23 meters $\times$ 20 meters = _____

12. 45 centimeters $\times$ 16 centimeters = _____

13. 12 millimeters $\times$ 100 millimeters = _____

14. 3.6 centimeters $\times$ 100 centimeters = _____

15. 0.35 meters $\times$ 1,000 meters = _____

Part C

Directions: If beaker A = 25 mL, beaker B = 38 mL, beaker C =
58 mL, and beaker D = 7 mL, find the volumes below.
Include the correct units.

16. beaker A $+$ beaker C = _____

17. beaker C $+$ beaker D = _____

18. The sum of beakers A, B, C, and D = _____

19. The difference of beakers A and C = _____

20. The difference of beakers B and D = _____

Crossword: Properties

Across

1. Measures liquid volume, a graduated _____ .
3. Amount of matter in an object
7. Place where scientists work
9. To wander
10. Opposite of *less*
13. Invisible gas that surrounds the earth
14. Scientists perform this to answer a question
16. Amount of space an object takes up
18. The rounded top surface of liquid in a cylinder
19. Measure of the earth's gravity on an object
20. Liquid needed for life

Down

1. The study of matter and how it changes
2. Unit of liquid volume in the metric system
3. Has mass and takes up space
4. Opposite of *sweet*
5. A type of dense soil
6. Unit of mass in the metric system
8. You are, I _____ .
11. What you do when you are hungry
12. A characteristic that helps identify something
14. Not odd
15. Used to measure weight
17. When counting, you start with _____ .

Compare and Contrast

Directions: When you compare and contrast things or ideas, you tell how they are alike and how they are different. Compare and contrast each pair below.

1. LENGTH—VOLUME
   a. How they are alike

_____

_____

_____

_____

   b. How they are different

_____

_____

_____

_____

2. CUBE—SPHERE
   a. How they are alike

_____

_____

_____

_____

   b. How they are different

_____

_____

_____

_____

3. WEIGHT—MASS
   a. How they are alike

_____

_____

_____

_____

   b. How they are different

_____

_____

_____

_____

4. BALANCE—GRADUATED CYLINDER
   a. How they are alike

_____

_____

_____

_____

   b. How they are different

_____

_____

_____

_____

5. PROPERTY—MEASUREMENT
   a. How they are alike

_____

_____

_____

_____

   b. How they are different

_____

_____

_____

Word Search: Matter

Directions: Write the correct word for each definition. As a check,
find each vocabulary word in the puzzle below.

1. the study of matter and how it changes _____

2. place where scientists conduct experiments _____

3. anything that has mass and takes up space _____

4. instrument used to measure mass _____

5. a measure of how strongly the earth's gravity attracts
something _____

6. a quality or characteristic that helps to identify a substance _____

7. a round glass or plastic container used to measure liquids
(two words) _____

8. the rounded top of a liquid seen in a graduated cylinder _____

9. one who studies matter and how it changes _____

10. a cube one centimeter on each side (two words) _____

Can you also find these words? *millimeter, volume*

```
E  D  V  R  C  B  H  T  F  K  O  G  M  D  L
S  U  H  Z  S  B  U  E  K  F  D  R  I  B  A
C  E  B  A  L  A  N  C  E  X  P  A  L  Y  B
H  C  E  N  T  I  M  E  T  E  R  D  L  P  O
E  Y  H  V  A  N  N  H  M  M  T  U  I  R  R
M  H  D  E  P  O  G  E  E  A  A  A  M  O  A
I  P  K  Z  M  I  H  R  N  T  V  T  E  P  T
S  C  Y  U  E  I  E  O  I  T  O  E  T  E  O
T  M  U  W  P  D  S  J  S  E  L  D  E  R  R
R  J  P  B  N  G  U  T  C  R  U  F  R  T  Y
Y  I  P  I  I  G  G  Z  U  V  M  C  S  Y  O
D  L  L  Z  A  C  Y  S  S  D  E  Q  L  S  V
U  Y  P  F  N  F  Q  T  V  P  Y  A  Y  M  G
C  P  Z  D  R  K  R  G  V  E  D  W  W  N  B
```

Science Terms Review

Part A

Directions: Match each term in Column A with its meaning in Column
B. Write the correct letter on the line.

Column A   **Column B**

_____ **1.** weight   **a.** Anything that has mass and takes up space

_____ **2.** chemistry   **b.** A cube one centimeter on each side, equal to one
                                              milliliter
_____ **3.** laboratory
                                          c. An instrument used to measure mass
_____ **4.** matter
                                          d. A measure of how strongly the earth's gravity
_____ **5.** balance   attracts something

_____ **6.** property   **e.** A place where scientists conduct experiments

_____ **7.** cubic centimeter **f.** A round glass or plastic cylinder used to measure
                                              liquids
_____ **8.** graduated cylinder
                                          g. The study of matter and how it changes

                                          h. A quality or characteristic that helps to identify
                                              a substance

Part B

Directions: Unscramble the word or words in parentheses to complete
each sentence below.

9. A _____ is one who studies chemistry.
        (mectish)

10. _____ equals length times width times height.
        (lumove)

11. One _____ equals 1/1,000 of a meter.
        (retemillim)

12. _____ is a property that tells how tightly matter is packed within a
        (estindy)   given volume.

Crossword: Matter

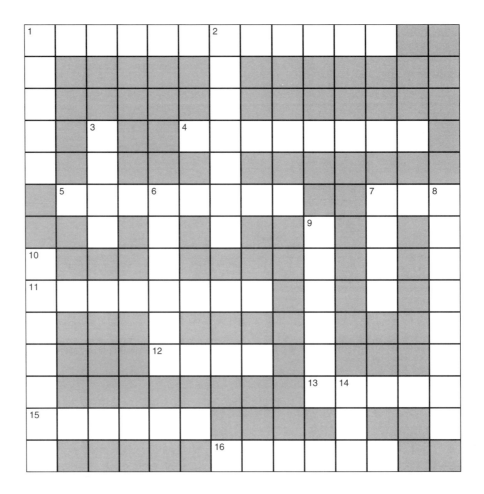

Across

1. Equals number of protons in an atom (two words)

4. There are 92 natural _____ .

5. Two or more elements combined chemically

7. Short for *Mother*

11. Particle with the symbol (−)

12. Element used in electric signs

13. Representation of how something looks or works

15. One of the elements in water

16. Takes up space and has mass

Down

1. All substances are made from these.

2. The central part of the atom

3. Element used to make steel

6. Particle with the symbol (+)

7. Equal to number of protons plus neutrons: _____ number

8. Smallest unit of a compound

9. Gas used in balloons

10. Particle in the nucleus; similar in size to electron

14. Atomic number of hydrogen

Compare and Contrast

Directions: When you compare and contrast things or ideas, you tell how they are alike and how they are different. Compare and contrast each pair below.

1. MOLECULE—ATOM
   a. How they are alike

   _____

   _____

   _____

   _____

   b. How they are different

   _____

   _____

   _____

   _____

2. ELEMENT—COMPOUND
   a. How they are alike

   _____

   _____

   _____

   _____

   b. How they are different

   _____

   _____

   _____

   _____

3. PROTON—ELECTRON
   a. How they are alike

   _____

   _____

   _____

   _____

   b. How they are different

   _____

   _____

   _____

   _____

4. NEUTRON—PROTON
   a. How they are alike

   _____

   _____

   _____

   _____

   b. How they are different

   _____

   _____

   _____

   _____

5. ATOMIC NUMBER—MASS NUMBER
   a. How they are alike

   _____

   _____

   _____

   _____

   b. How they are different

   _____

   _____

   _____

   _____

Solids, Liquids, and Gases

Part A
Directions: Use the diagrams to complete the following statements.

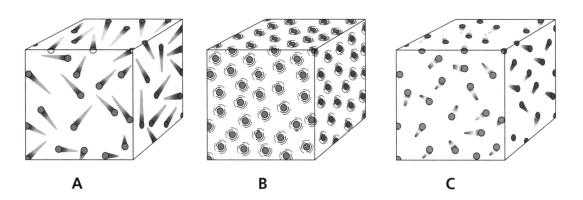

A   **B**   **C**

1. The diagrams show _____ for three states of matter.

2. Liquids are best represented by Diagram _____ .

3. Gases are best represented by Diagram _____ .

4. Diagram _____ shows the state of matter with the greatest density.

5. One state of matter that is not represented by the diagrams is _____ .

Part B
Directions: Match each item with the diagram that best represents it.
Write the letter of the diagram in the space provided.

6. ice cube _____

7. skateboard _____

8. feather _____

9. helium in a balloon _____

10. raindrop _____

11. gold ring _____

12. orange juice _____

13. cotton candy _____

14. air _____

15. neon in a sign _____

Matter: Terms Review

Part A

Directions: Match each term in Column A with its meaning in Column B. Write the correct letter on the line.

Column A

_____ **1.** molecule

_____ **2.** atom

_____ **3.** element

_____ **4.** electron

_____ **5.** neutron

_____ **6.** nucleus

_____ **7.** mass number

_____ **8.** plasma

Column B

a. One of 92 natural substances that are the basic building blocks of matter

b. Equal to the number of protons plus the number of neutrons in an atom

c. Very hot gas made of charged particles

d. A particle found in the nucleus of an atom

e. A particle with a negative charge

f. The smallest particle of a compound; made of one or more atoms

g. The building block of matter

Part B

Directions: Unscramble the word or words in parentheses to complete each sentence below.

9. An _____ is a number that is equal to the number of protons in an atom.
      (mactoi murben)

10. A _____ is a substance made of two or more elements combined chemically.
       (modoncup)

11. A _____ is a particle found in the nucleus of an atom.
        (troonp)

12. The mass of an element is related to its _____ .
        (sams murben)

Crossword: Elements

Across

1. List of all of the elements in columns and rows (two words)
5. Type of elements; gold is an example.
7. Its symbol is B.
8. Mass divided by volume
10. Helium is a noble _____ .
12. Opposite of *no*
14. Group of elements in the same column
15. Type of element with properties that are different from a metal
17. Its symbol is Pt.

Down

2. Deuterium is an _____ of hydrogen.
3. Does not ordinarily react.
4. Its symbol is Pb.
6. A mixture of two or more metals
7. Its symbol is Br.
8. An isotope of hydrogen with one neutron
9. An isotope of hydrogen with two neutrons
11. Abbreviation for element's name
13. Its symbol is S.
14. Enjoyable
16. Its symbol is Sn.

Compare and Contrast

Directions: When you compare and contrast things or ideas, you tell how they are alike and how they are different. Compare and contrast each pair below.

1. CHEMICAL SYMBOL—ABBREVIATION
a. How they are alike

_____

_____

_____

_____

b. How they are different

_____

_____

_____

_____

2. ROW—COLUMN
a. How they are alike

_____

_____

_____

_____

b. How they are different

_____

_____

_____

_____

3. HYDROGEN—DEUTERIUM
a. How they are alike

_____

_____

_____

_____

b. How they are different

_____

_____

_____

_____

4. SOLDER—BRONZE
a. How they are alike

_____

_____

_____

_____

b. How they are different

_____

_____

_____

_____

5. METALS—NONMETALS
a. How they are alike

_____

_____

_____

_____

b. How they are different

_____

_____

_____

_____

Words From Chemical Symbols

Directions: Read the clue in Column A. You can find the answer from the elements in Column B. In Column C, write the symbols for the elements in Column B. The word you form should be the correct answer for the clue. The first one is done for you.

A	B	C
1. A farm animal	cobalt-tungsten	CoW
2. A person who doesn't tell the truth	lithium-argon	_____
3. The opposite of *lose*	tungsten-iodine-nitrogen	_____
4. A building material	bromine-iodine-carbon-potassium	_____
5. Found on a door	potassium-nitrogen-oxygen-boron	_____
6. Used to write on a blackboard	carbon-hydrogen-aluminum-potassium	_____
7. A dog's sound	boron-argon-potassium	_____
8. It's 150 million km away	sulfur-uranium-nitrogen	_____
9. A source of energy	cobalt-aluminum	_____
10. A funny person	chlorine-oxygen-tungsten-nitrogen	_____
11. Used in hockey	plutonium-carbon-potassium	_____
12. A cow's offspring	carbon-aluminum-fluorine	_____
13. A form of money	cobalt-iodine-nitrogen	_____
14. Show of affection	potassium-iodine-sulfur-sulfur	_____
15. Another word for *ill*	silicon-carbon-potassium	_____
16. The saint who visits on Christmas Eve	nickel-carbon-potassium	_____
17. A form of transportation	calcium-boron	_____
18. To make better	helium-aluminum	_____
19. King of the beasts	lithium-oxygen-nitrogen	_____
20. A form of precipitation	radium-iodine-nitrogen	_____

Word Search: Elements

Directions: Write the correct word for each definition. As a check, find each vocabulary word in the puzzle below.

1. an abbreviation for the name of an element _____

2. a table that lists the elements in order of increasing atomic number (two words) _____

3. a mixture of two or more metals _____

4. a form of an element that has the same number of protons and electrons but a different number of neutrons _____

5. elements on the right side of the periodic table that are not good conductors of heat and electricity _____

6. the mass of an object divided by its volume _____

7. a group of elements on the left side of the periodic table that are usually shiny and are good conductors of heat and electricity _____

8. a group of gases that do not react with other substances under ordinary conditions (two words) _____

9. a word that describes noble gases _____

```
N  K  N  O  J  Y  E  A  N  D  V  R  C  B  H
O  T  F  K  O  D  S  L  B  S  U  H  I  Z  S
N  B  N  E  K  F  D  L  B  Y  B  E  S  Y  V
M  A  O  N  P  T  H  O  E  M  D  P  O  O  E
E  A  B  K  E  Z  H  Y  H  B  U  O  T  M  P
T  J  L  P  R  G  U  F  G  O  I  P  O  G  G
A  Z  E  C  I  T  S  O  A  L  D  L  P  Z  A
L  Y  G  D  O  I  A  Q  Z  L  S  L  E  Y  V
S  P  A  N  D  N  F  B  X  O  A  T  T  V  P
Y  A  S  M  I  E  G  P  L  T  Z  I  D  R  K
R  G  E  E  C  R  D  W  D  E  S  W  N  B  F
X  M  S  K  H  T  B  W  S  N  W  D  Z  U  N
E  L  Z  X  W  K  L  M  E  H  H  P  T  H  N
M  E  T  A  L  S  H  D  X  X  M  E  N  J  D
```

Elements: Terms Review

Part A

Directions: Match each term in Column A with its meaning in
Column B. Write the correct letter on the line.

Column A	Column B
_____ **1.** periodic table	**a.** A group of gases that do not react with other substances under ordinary conditions
_____ **2.** alloy	
_____ **3.** nonmetals	**b.** Form of an element; having the same number of protons and electrons but a different number of neutrons
_____ **4.** atomic mass	
_____ **5.** deuterium	**c.** A group of elements with similar properties arranged in a column on the periodic table
_____ **6.** isotope	
_____ **7.** noble gases	**d.** The average mass of all the isotopes of an element
_____ **8.** family	
	e. A table that lists the elements in order of increasing atomic number
	f. A mixture of two or more metals
	g. Elements found on the right side of the periodic table, which are not good conductors of heat or electricity
	h. A form of hydrogen

Part B

Directions: Unscramble the word or words in parentheses to
complete each sentence below.

9. A _____ is an abbreviation for the name of an element.
   (mobsly)

10. _____ are the elements placed on the left side of the periodic table.
   (saltem)   They are usually shiny and are good conductors of heat and
   electricity.

11. _____ gases will not combine with other substances under ordinary
   (entir)   conditions.

12. _____ is an isotope of hydrogen.
   (riimutt)

Math Connection: Atomic Number Puzzle

Directions: Write the atomic number for the element in each square.
Then add the five atomic numbers in each row and in
each column. Write the sums. If your atomic numbers
are correct, the sums will all be the same.

Fe	As	Ne	Cl	Cr	Sums
_____	_____	_____	_____	_____	_____
Ge	Si	S	V	Mn	
_____	_____	_____	_____	_____	_____
Al	P	Ti	Cu	Ga	
_____	_____	_____	_____	_____	_____
K	Sc	Ni	Zn	Mg	
_____	_____	_____	_____	_____	_____
Ca	Co	Se	Na	Ar	
_____	_____	_____	_____	_____	_____

Sums

_____   _____   _____   _____   _____

Crossword: Compounds

Across

1. _____ are contained in energy levels
4. Reacts with a metal to form hydrogen
6. An atom that has a charge
8. Small number written below a symbol in a chemical formula
10. Symbol for magnesium
13. They identify acids and bases.
14. A kind of chemical recipe
17. Particle with no charge

Down

1. Hydrogen is a natural _____, one of 92.
2. Chemical combination of two or more elements
3. Li
5. Has a bitter taste
7. NO_3
9. OH is an example of one.
11. State of matter
12. C
15. Opposite of *in*
16. A cow's sound

Compare and Contrast

Directions: When you compare and contrast things or ideas, you tell how they are alike and how they are different. Compare and contrast each pair below.

1. SUBSCRIPT—SYMBOL
   a. How they are alike

   _____
   _____
   _____
   _____

   b. How they are different

   _____
   _____
   _____
   _____

2. PHYSICAL CHANGE—CHEMICAL CHANGE
   a. How they are alike

   _____
   _____
   _____
   _____

   b. How they are different

   _____
   _____
   _____
   _____

3. FORMULA—RECIPE
   a. How they are alike

   _____
   _____
   _____
   _____

   b. How they are different

   _____
   _____
   _____
   _____

4. ACIDS—BASES
   a. How they are alike

   _____
   _____
   _____
   _____

   b. How they are different

   _____
   _____
   _____
   _____

5. ION—ATOM
   a. How they are alike

   _____
   _____
   _____
   _____

   b. How they are different

   _____
   _____
   _____
   _____

Interpreting Chemical Formulas

Part A

Directions: Write the chemical formula for each compound described. Find the chemical symbols in the periodic table.

1. silver chloride = one atom of silver + one atom of chlorine

_____

2. hydrochloric acid = one atom of hydrogen + one atom of chlorine

_____

3. hydrogen peroxide = two atoms of hydrogen + two atoms of oxygen

_____

4. magnesium carbonate = one atom of magnesium + one atom of carbon + three atoms of oxygen

_____

5. glucose = six atoms of carbon + twelve atoms of hydrogen + six atoms of oxygen

_____

6. lead nitrate = one atom of lead + two nitrate radicals

_____

Part B

Directions: Complete the table. Name the elements in each compound, and tell how many atoms of each element there are.

Compound	Elements	Atoms
7. potassium chloride, KCl		
8. sucrose, $C_{12}H_{22}O_{11}$		
9. ammonium bromide, NH_4Br		
10. ammonium carbonate, $(NH_4)_2CO_3$		

Word Search: Compounds

Directions: Write the correct word for each definition. As a check, find each vocabulary word in the puzzle below.

1. a compound that reacts with metals to form hydrogen _____

2. a group of two or more atoms that act like one element _____

3. an abbreviation for compounds telling what elements and how many atoms of each element the compound contains _____

4. a compound containing the hydroxyl radical _____

5. a space at a certain distance from the nucleus of the atom in which electrons move (two words) _____

6. a charged atom _____

7. an acid found in vinegar _____

8. a chemical combination of two or more elements _____

9. a radical containing nitrogen and oxygen _____

10. a number following a chemical symbol that tells how many atoms of an element there are in a compound _____

```
E  Z  K  N  U  Q  D  I  J  L  R  T  E  S  I
A  B  M  R  A  S  S  V  A  W  Z  S  L  T  C
N  Q  J  U  S  C  C  C  B  B  J  B  V  M  E
S  U  B  S  C  R  I  P  T  S  L  A  C  I  C
X  D  I  I  Y  D  X  D  Q  E  L  Q  A  T  O
L  V  Y  D  A  S  Z  W  V  U  L  P  N  F  M
E  Z  W  R  Z  Z  H  E  M  W  I  T  S  A  P
Y  H  B  H  Q  A  L  R  L  B  M  U  C  Y  O
M  Y  A  E  E  Y  O  P  I  O  N  A  M  Y  U
H  J  S  X  G  F  Q  O  P  K  Y  Q  L  I  N
B  A  Z  R  R  Z  O  U  E  F  Z  H  E  I  D
B  F  E  I  Q  V  N  I  T  R  A  T  E  C  H
M  N  P  U  N  A  F  P  G  G  Q  C  W  M  M
E  A  C  E  T  I  C  M  Y  W  Q  N  P  V  J
```

Compounds: Terms Review

Part A
Directions: Match each term in Column A with its meaning in Column
B. Write the correct letter on the line.

Column A   **Column B**

_____ **1.** subscript

_____ **2.** radical

_____ **3.** ion

_____ **4.** base

_____ **5.** acid

_____ **6.** formula

_____ **7.** energy levels

_____ **8.** pH

a. A sour-tasting compound that reacts with metals to form hydrogen

b. Spaces surrounding the nucleus of the atom in which electrons move

c. Number that tells whether a substance is an acid or a base

d. An abbreviation for compounds telling what elements and how many atoms of each element the compound contains

e. A charged atom

f. A bitter-tasting compound containing the OH radical

g. Number used in formulas to tell how many atoms of an element make up a unit of the compound

h. A group of two or more elements that acts like one element

Part B
Directions: Unscramble the word or words in parentheses to complete
each sentence below.

9. The _____ radical contains sulfur and oxygen.
             (alsetfu)

10. A _____ is a change in which new substances with new properties are
       (himaccel gnache)   formed.

11. _____ , carbon, and oxygen are combined in the compound K_2CO_3.
       (smiopauts)

12. A _____ holds atoms together in a compound.
       (machicle nobd)

Crossword: Reactions

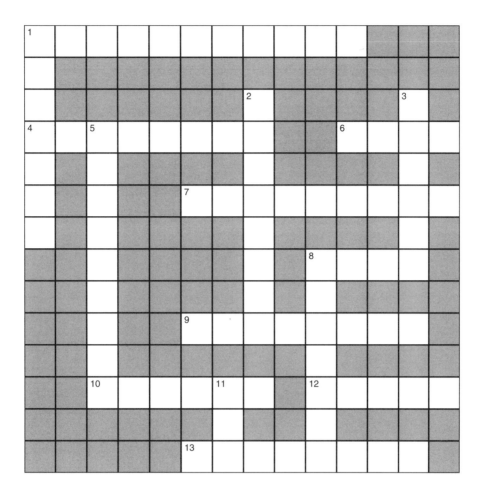

Across

1. Solid formed in a reaction

4. To break apart into particles

6. Not sweet

7. Someone who would try to change substances into gold

8. In the near future

9. Used for heating (two words)

10. Substance that dissolves

12. In a balanced equation, the number of atoms on both sides are _____ .

13. Mixture formed by dissolving one substance in another

Down

1. Formed by a reaction

2. Shown on the left side of a chemical equation

3. A type of burner

5. A reaction in which two elements combine to form a compound

8. Substance in which dissolving occurs

11. Also

Compare and Contrast

Directions: When you compare and contrast things or ideas, you tell how they are alike and how they are different. Compare and contrast each pair below.

1. MIXTURE—SOLUTION
   a. How they are alike

_____

_____

_____

_____

   b. How they are different

_____

_____

_____

_____

2. SYNTHESIS REACTION—
   DECOMPOSITION REACTION
   a. How they are alike

_____

_____

_____

_____

   b. How they are different

_____

_____

_____

_____

3. REACTANT—PRODUCT
   a. How they are alike

_____

_____

_____

_____

   b. How they are different

_____

_____

_____

_____

4. COEFFICIENT—SUBSCRIPT
   a. How they are alike

_____

_____

_____

_____

   b. How they are different

_____

_____

_____

_____

5. SOLUTE—SOLVENT
   a. How they are alike

_____

_____

_____

_____

   b. How they are different

_____

_____

_____

_____

Interpreting Chemical Equations

Part A

Directions: For each of the following chemical equations, tell what type of reaction it is.

1. $2H_2 = O_2 \rightarrow 2H_2O$ _____

2. $2MgO \rightarrow 2Mg + O^2$ _____

3. $Zn + 2HCl \rightarrow ZnCl^2 + H^2$ _____

4. $2KClO_3 \rightarrow 2KCl + 3O_2$ _____

Part B

Directions: Identify the reactants and product in the following reaction.

$$4Al + 3O_2 \rightarrow 2Al_2O_3$$

5. reactants: _____

6. product: _____

Part C

Directions: Use the following chemical equation to answer questions 7 through 12.

$$2AgNO_3 + BaI_2 \rightarrow Ba(NO_3)_2 + 2AgI$$

7. What are the reactants? _____

8. What are the products? _____

9. How many atoms of barium are on both sides of the equation?

_____

10. How many atoms of iodine are on both sides of the equation?

_____

11. How many atoms of silver are on both sides of the equation? How do you know?

_____

12. What type of reaction is this?

_____

Word Search: Reactions

Directions: Write the correct word for each description. As a check,
find each vocabulary word in the puzzle below.

1. person who tried to change various substances into gold
   and other precious metals _____

2. chemical change _____

3. type of chemical reaction in which two or more elements
   combine to form one compound (one word) _____

4. statement that uses symbols and formulas to describe
   a chemical reaction (two words) _____

5. a substance in a reaction shown on the left side of a
   chemical equation _____

6. a number placed before a chemical formula that
   indicates the number of molecules in a chemical equation _____

7. a substance that is formed during a reaction; shown on
   the right side of the arrow in a chemical equation _____

8. part of a solution in which a substance dissolves _____

9. solid that forms in a solution _____

10. combination of substances in which neither substance
    changes _____

```
C F Z Q M X T X O R E A C T A N T G
H B P E O C O E F F I C I E N T D S
E C N M L L O H U E F Y O I S T L I
M Q C A E T A T I P I C E R P R L A
I P U Q D N M K G O W O I V C T R L
C R P A N L V Q O L C X F C S E Q H
A O S K T F I L G M U J O I I L P J
L D W Y M I X T U R E T M S P E K E
F U E X N G O I L Z K E V B E X N F
Q C D O K T W N E X H T I P H J B T
P T I O L U H R S C D N O O X Z L T
A X N F L W D E L O S O L V E N T U
E W Y W Y D H A S Y N T H E S I P
W R E A C T I O N I A V Q Y Q T G X
```

Reactions: Terms Review

Part A
Directions: Match each term in Column A with its meaning in
Column B. Write the correct letter on the line.

Column A

_____ **1.** alchemist

_____ **2.** synthesis reaction

_____ **3.** reactant

_____ **4.** coefficient

_____ **5.** reaction

_____ **6.** chemical equation

_____ **7.** solute

_____ **8.** balance

Column B

a. Any chemical change

b. A statement that uses symbols and formulas to describe a chemical reaction

c. A substance that dissolves in a solution

d. A substance that enters into a reaction; found on the left side of the arrow in a chemical equation

e. How you make the number of atoms the same on both sides of a chemical equation

f. A person who tried to change various substances into gold and other precious metals

g. A chemical reaction in which two or more elements combine to form one compound

h. A number placed before a chemical formula, which indicates the number of molecules in a chemical equation

Part B
Directions: Unscramble the word or words in parentheses to complete
each sentence below.

9. A _____ is a substance that is formed during a reaction and shown on
(cuptrod)   the right side of a chemical equation.

10. A _____ is the substance in which a solute dissolves.
(novlest)

11. The law of _____ of matter states that matter cannot be created or
(introvosance)   destroyed.

12. A _____ is one kind of mixture.
(oilsnout)

Compare and Contrast

Directions: When you compare and contrast things or ideas, you tell
how they are alike and how they are different. Compare
and contrast each pair below.

1. SPEED—VELOCITY
   a. How they are alike

_____

_____

_____

_____

   b. How they are different

_____

_____

_____

_____

2. INERTIA—FRICTION
   a. How they are alike

_____

_____

_____

_____

   b. How they are different

_____

_____

_____

_____

3. DISTANCE—ELAPSED TIME
   a. How they are alike

_____

_____

_____

_____

   b. How they are different

_____

_____

_____

_____

4. MOTION—ACCELERATION
   a. How they are alike

_____

_____

_____

_____

   b. How they are different

_____

_____

_____

_____

5. GRAVITY—AIR RESISTANCE
   a. How they are alike

_____

_____

_____

_____

   b. How they are different

_____

_____

_____

_____

Word Search: Force and Motion

Directions: Write the correct word for each definition. As a check, find each vocabulary word in the puzzle below.

1. the change in speed divided by the change in time _____

2. a push or a pull _____

3. a force that opposes motion _____

4. the force of attraction between any two objects that have mass _____

5. the distance traveled per unit of time _____

6. change in position _____

7. tendency to resist changes in motion _____

8. speed and direction _____

9. equals distance divided by speed _____

10. equals speed times time _____ _____

```
S  D  A  C  C  E  L  E  R  A  T  I  O  N  H
O  P  W  J  T  S  M  Y  A  T  X  J  O  N  L
D  J  E  R  T  P  I  O  X  A  V  I  O  T  D
S  M  L  E  O  D  I  N  I  B  F  I  M  O  G
O  O  W  W  D  B  R  T  X  N  T  W  R  W  R
A  T  M  L  H  E  R  S  S  C  R  B  V  P  A
M  I  V  B  L  E  E  C  I  V  S  E  L  O  V
Z  O  E  K  N  D  B  R  V  E  L  X  V  P  I
M  N  K  I  A  T  F  R  G  O  Y  O  U  R  T
V  S  C  X  P  H  S  A  C  F  O  R  C  E  Y
H  E  K  F  K  X  R  I  M  I  Z  J  G  S  W
D  K  L  T  Y  E  T  D  I  S  T  A  N  C  E
J  T  I  M  E  Y  S  E  Z  S  I  P  Y  U  G
```

Force and Motion: Terms Review

Part A
Directions: Match each term in Column A with a phrase in Column B.
Write the correct letter on the line.

Column A   **Column B**

_____ **1.** inertia   **a.** The tendency to resist change in motion

_____ **2.** acceleration   **b.** A push or a pull

_____ **3.** friction   **c.** The distance traveled per unit of time

_____ **4.** gravity   **d.** The time that passes between one event and another

_____ **5.** velocity   **e.** The change in speed divided by the change in time

_____ **6.** force   **f.** A force that opposes motion

_____ **7.** speed   **g.** The force of attraction between any two objects that
                                     have mass
_____ **8.** elapsed time
                                h. Speed and direction of a moving object

Part B
Directions: Unscramble the word or words in parentheses to complete
each sentence below.

9. The _____ of a moving object tells the direction of motion as well as
(yetlovic)   the speed.

10. A _____ has no acceleration.
(cannots deeps)

11. _____ equals the product of speed and time.
(candetis)

12. The law of _____ states that gravity depends on mass and distance.
(savenuril tatairoving)

Math Connection: Calculating Speed

Speed is calculated by dividing the distance by the time.

$$speed = \frac{distance}{time}$$

Directions: Solve for the speed in each of the following problems. Include the correct unit in your answer.

1. speed = $\dfrac{120 \text{ millimeters}}{60 \text{ seconds}}$ _____

2. speed = $\dfrac{400 \text{ meters}}{80 \text{ seconds}}$ _____

3. speed = $\dfrac{700 \text{ centimeters}}{35 \text{ seconds}}$ _____

4. speed = $\dfrac{1{,}000 \text{ meters}}{100 \text{ seconds}}$ _____

5. speed = $\dfrac{12.5 \text{ millimeters}}{0.5 \text{ seconds}}$ _____

6. speed = $\dfrac{0.045 \text{ meters}}{0.05 \text{ seconds}}$ _____

7. speed = $\dfrac{0.015 \text{ millimeters}}{0.10 \text{ seconds}}$ _____

8. speed = $\dfrac{10.4 \text{ centimeters}}{10.0 \text{ seconds}}$ _____

9. Solve for the speed if the distance is 200 meters and the time is 50 seconds.

   _____

10. Solve for the speed if the distance is 230 meters and the time is 45 seconds.

    _____

11. Solve for the speed if the distance is 155 meters and the time is 10.0 seconds.

    _____

12. Solve for the speed if the distance is 12.6 meters and the time is 0.3 seconds.

    _____

13. Solve for the speed if the distance is 0.34 meters and the time is 0.17 seconds.

    _____

14. Solve for the speed if the distance is 0.50 meters and the time is 10 seconds.

    _____

Math Connection: Interpreting a Graph

Directions: Study this graph. It shows the distance traveled by three vehicles traveling at constant speeds. Use the graph to complete the table that follows.

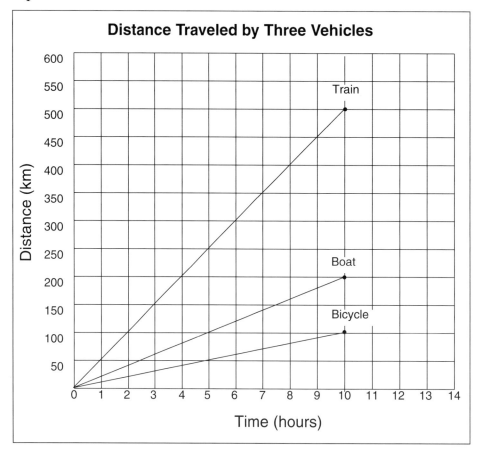

Elapsed Time in Hours	Distance Traveled in Kilometers		
	Boat	Train	Bicycle
1			
2			
3			
4			
5			
6			
7			
8			
9			
10			

What is the speed of each vehicle? _____

_____

Math Connection: Constructing a Graph

Directions: Use the data in this table to complete the graph that follows. Plot the distance traveled for each of the three vehicles.

Elapsed Time in Hours	Distance Traveled in Kilometers		
	Car	Motorcycle	Train
1	75	25	50
2	150	50	100
3	225	75	150
4	300	100	200
5	375	125	250

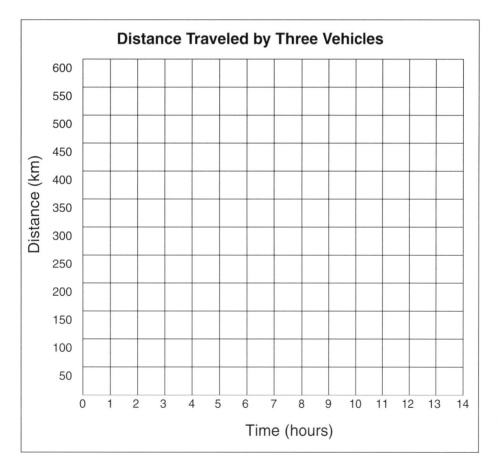

1. How would you describe the motion of all three vehicles? _____

2. How far would each vehicle travel in 6 hours at the same speed? _____

Crossword: Work

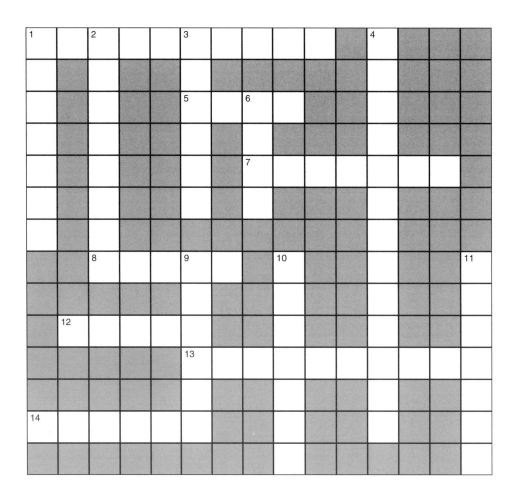

Across

1. A form of energy produced by a machine
5. Force times distance
7. A simple _____ makes work easier.
8. A broom is one example.
12. Metric unit of work
13. The object that is moved by a machine
14. A wheel and a rope together

Down

1. One type of pulley
2. The type of energy a battery stores
3. Metric unit of force
4. Simple machine with no moving parts (two words)
6. Another word for inclined plane
9. Ability to do work
10. Form of energy received from the sun
11. Energy of motion

Compare and Contrast

Directions: When you compare and contrast things or ideas, you tell
how they are alike and how they are different. Compare
and contrast each pair below.

1. NEWTON—JOULE
   a. How they are alike

_____

_____

_____

_____

   b. How they are different

_____

_____

_____

_____

2. KINETIC ENERGY—POTENTIAL
   ENERGY
   a. How they are alike

_____

_____

_____

_____

   b. How they are different

_____

_____

_____

_____

3. EFFORT FORCE—RESISTANCE FORCE
   a. How they are alike

_____

_____

_____

_____

   b. How they are different

_____

_____

_____

_____

4. RAKE—WHEELBARROW
   a. How they are alike

_____

_____

_____

_____

   b. How they are different

_____

_____

_____

5. LEVER—PULLEY
   a. How they are alike

_____

_____

_____

   b. How they are different

_____

_____

_____

Word Search: Work

Directions: Write the correct word for each definition. As a check,
find each vocabulary word in the puzzle below.

1. a quantity found by multiplying the force by the
distance moved   _____

2. a device used to measure force (two words)   _____

3. the metric unit of work   _____

4. the energy of motion (two words)   _____

5. the unit of force in the metric system   _____

6. an inclined plane   _____

7. device that changes mechanical energy to electrical energy   _____

8. ability to do work   _____

9. the energy of position; stored energy   _____

10. a device that makes work easier by changing the
direction of a force (two words)   _____

Can you also find the word *lever*?

```
J E G V Y S X J J V E W P A L K
U Q W G P S V B N L H D A V N I
U P N U O U P N A V R E Z R E N
C Z O P Q K B C X A Z R A S N E
P L V T Q E S N J O V V Z B E T
G H B A E G G D B T L E U C R I
O L Z G N N P E N E W T O N G C
F E E I Y M T K N P J F X J Y E
S L R V A A I I O E K R M O Y N
I P K R E N A F A X R P Z U O E
S R K P T R T B U L A A X L K R
O O G L C H N P O Q E J T E M G
S I M P L E M A C H I N E O W Y
A Y C S O N G R O N B V E S R O
K C Z O Y X N V C H A W R R O O
W R D W O R K V R R U K A Z G J
R V V B J X G Y Z X A Y N B U Y
```

Work: Terms Review

Part A

Directions: Match each term in Column A with its meaning in Column B. Write the correct letter on the line.

Column A	Column B
_____ **1.** spring scale	**a.** A device that changes the size or direction of a force or the distance over which a force acts
_____ **2.** kinetic energy	**b.** A bar that turns about a fulcrum
_____ **3.** newton	**c.** The energy of position; stored energy
_____ **4.** lever	**d.** The energy of motion
_____ **5.** ramp	**e.** A device used to measure force
_____ **6.** potential energy	**f.** Also called an inclined plane
_____ **7.** simple machine	**g.** The unit of force in the metric system

Part B

Directions: Unscramble the word or words in parentheses to complete each sentence below.

8. _____ is what happens when a force makes something move
    (kwor)

9. The _____ is the metric unit of work.
    (lujoe)

10. A _____ is a point about which a lever moves.
    (murcluf)

11. _____ is the ability to do work.
    (eeryng)

12. A _____ is a device that converts mechanical energy to electrical
    (reenactrong)   energy.

Machines: Terms Review

Part A
Directions: Match each term in Column A with its meaning in Column
B. Write the correct letter on the line.

Column A

_____ **1.** effort force

_____ **2.** resistance force

_____ **3.** movable pulley

_____ **4.** inclined plane

_____ **5.** wedge

_____ **6.** mechanical
advantage

_____ **7.** fixed pulley

Column B

a. A type of simple machine that is used like a ramp

b. The number of times by which a machine multiplies
effort force

c. A pulley that does not move as the resistance moves

d. A pulley that is not attached to a stationary object
and is therefore free to move

e. The force that is applied to a simple machine

f. An inclined plane that is made to move in order to
move the resistance

g. The force applied by the resistance

Part B
Directions: Unscramble the word or words in parentheses to complete
each sentence below.

8. A _____ is the point around which a lever rotates.
(cruflum)

9. A _____ is a simple machine consisting of a wheel with a rope, string,
(uplely)   or chain that wraps around the wheel.

10. A _____ is an inclined plane.
(marp)

11. The _____ is the distance between the fulcrum and the resistance force.
(tetrof mar)

Math Connection: Calculating Work

Work = Force applied × distance moved
or
Work = F × d

Part A

Directions: Solve the following problems.

1. work = 10 newtons × 23 meters

= _____

2. work = 22 newtons × 15 meters

= _____

3. work = 38 newtons × 11 meters

= _____

4. work = 12.6 newtons × 2.0 meters

= _____

5. work = 120 newtons × 6 meters

= _____

6. work = 100 newtons × 0.5 meter

= _____

7. work = 20 newtons × 3.0 meters

= _____

8. work = 25 newtons × 1.0 meter

= _____

9. work = 3.2 newtons × 5.0 meters

= _____

10. work = 0.5 newtons × 1.5 meters

= _____

11. work = 0.75 newtons × 0.50 meter

= _____

12. work = 1.5 newtons × 0.75 meter

= _____

Part B

Directions: Solve the following problems. Convert units where
necessary.

13. A teacher pushes a bookshelf, using a force of 10 newtons. If the teacher moved the bookshelf 20 feet, how much work did she do?

work = _____

14. A woman lifts a package, using a force of 3.0 newtons. If she lifts the package 5.5 feet, how much work will be done?

work = _____

15. A boy pulls a wagon with a force of 8.5 newtons. If he moves the wagon 18 feet, how much work will be done?

work = _____

16. A worker pulls a desk, using a force of 20 newtons. If he moves the desk 13 feet, how much work will be done?

work = _____

Crossword: Heat Energy

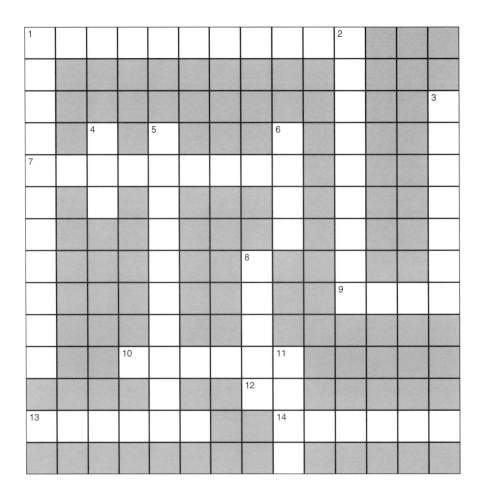

Across

1. Measures temperature
7. To change from liquid to gas
9. Three times three
10. Becomes solid above the melting point
12. To perform an action
13. To get larger when heated
14. Space with no matter

Down

1. Measurement of how fast the particles of a substance are moving
2. Energy carried across space
3. Unit of heat
4. Produced by evaporation
5. Heat transfer by bumping molecules
6. Results from the motion of particles in matter
8. Becomes liquid below the freezing point
11. A type of bird

Compare and Contrast

Directions: When you compare and contrast things or ideas, you tell how they are alike and how they are different. Compare and contrast each pair below.

1. ICE—LIQUID WATER
  a. How they are alike

_____

_____

_____

_____

  b. How they are different

_____

_____

_____

_____

2. FAHRENHEIT SCALE—CELSIUS SCALE
  a. How they are alike

_____

_____

_____

_____

  b. How they are different

_____

_____

_____

_____

3. FREEZING POINT—MELTING POINT
  a. How they are alike

_____

_____

_____

_____

  b. How they are different

_____

_____

_____

_____

4. HEAT—TEMPERATURE
  a. How they are alike

_____

_____

_____

_____

  b. How they are different

_____

_____

_____

_____

5. RADIATION—CONDUCTION
  a. How they are alike

_____

_____

_____

_____

  b. How they are different

_____

_____

_____

_____

Heat Energy: Applying Ideas

Directions: Answer the following questions in the space provided.

1. Suppose you are trying to open a jar, but the lid won't turn. The lid is metal. Someone suggests running hot water over the lid. Would that help? Explain why or why not.

   _____

   _____

2. In the diagram, a mass is hanging from a wire. When the wire is heated as shown, will the mass move up or down? Why?

   _____

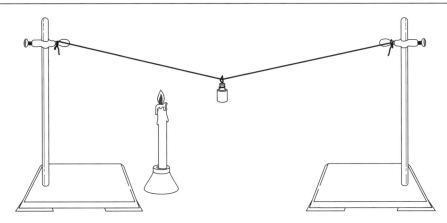

3. Suppose there are two bowls of hot soup with spoons in them. One spoon is plastic and the other is metal. Which spoon would feel hotter? Why?

   _____

   _____

4. Suppose you put a pan of water outside in a field on a clear day. If you measured the water's temperature at different times of day, when would you expect to get the highest reading? Why?

   _____

   _____

5. One problem that fireplace designers try to solve is how to get more of the fire's heat into the room. Where does the rest of the heat go? Why?

   _____

   _____

Word Search: Heat Energy

Directions: Write the correct word for each definition. As a check, find each vocabulary word in the puzzle below.

1. a type of energy caused by the motion of molecules _____

2. heat transfer resulting from rising particles in heated matter _____

3. results from a change at the melting point _____

4. to change from a liquid to a gas _____

5. results from a change at the boiling point _____

6. a measure of the average motion of the molecules in a substance _____

7. a device that measures temperature _____

8. the temperature scale on which water boils at 212 degrees _____

9. the temperature scale used in most of the world and for scientific work _____

10. the temperature at which a solid changes to a liquid (two words) _____

Can you also find the term *boiling point*?

```
G F F O Z M O L G V N W L T R
X H P A P E L B N L T J F P T
F Y G M H W V U O N A A L N N
R O R T E R J A O E L S I U S
F P T T H L E I P F Z O Q C M
M P A E E E T N X O P S U S M
Z E O E M C R I H G R M I L W
H C K J E P L M N E G A D E E
T O K V P B E I O G I Q T C P
J J N S E J L R E M P T V E J
M O E Z O I Y H A M E O I O W
C G A S O L A T H T J T I J P
O U U B W O L U O L U T E N K
F L E Z V E O J O O S R M R T
G L C F L G J S U I S L E C G
```

Heat Energy: Terms Review

Part A
Directions: Match each term in Column A with its meaning in
Column B. Write the correct letter on the line.

Column A

_____ **1.** calorie

_____ **2.** temperature

_____ **3.** convection

_____ **4.** Fahrenheit

_____ **5.** evaporate

_____ **6.** insulator

_____ **7.** melting point

Column B

a. To change from a liquid to a gas

b. Temperature at which a solid changes into a liquid

c. A material that does not conduct heat well

d. The amount of heat needed to raise the temperature of 1 g of water 1°C

e. A measure of the average motion of the molecules in a substance; It is measured with a thermometer.

f. The temperature scale commonly used in the United States

g. The heat transfer by rising warm particles

Part B
Directions: Unscramble the word or words in parentheses to complete
each sentence below.

8. A _____ is space without matter.
(camuvu)

9. _____ is one of the states of matter. Water is an example of this state.
(duqili)

10. _____ is the flow of heat energy through matter by molecules bumping
(noitcudonc) into each other.

11. _____ is the temperature scale used in scientific work.
(cussile)

Crossword: Sound and Light

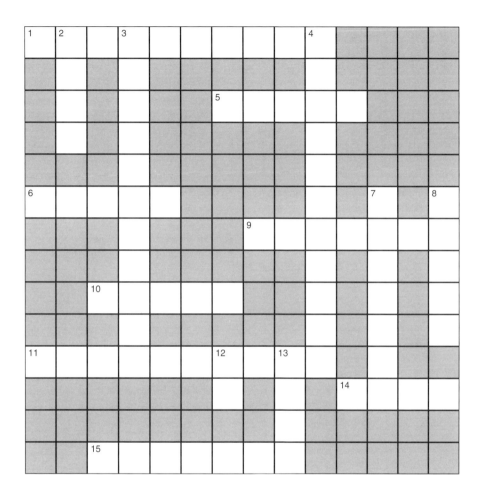

Across

1. Bending of light waves
5. Finds distance of underwater objects
6. Highness or lowness of sounds
9. What a convex lens will do to an image
10. The _____ point is where reflected or refracted light rays come together.
11. Can't see close-up objects clearly
14. Bends light waves to form an image
15. These reflect light waves to form an image

Down

2. A sound reflected to its source
3. Images formed by the bouncing back of light waves
4. Can't see distant objects clearly
7. To move rapidly back and forth
8. One complete back-and-forth motion
12. Abbreviation for *Hertz*
13. Organs used to detect sound

Compare and Contrast

Directions: When you compare and contrast things or ideas, you tell how they are alike and how they are different. Compare and contrast each pair below.

1. FREQUENCY—PITCH
   a. How they are alike

   _____
   _____
   _____
   _____

   b. How they are different

   _____
   _____
   _____
   _____

2. REFLECTION—REFRACTION
   a. How they are alike

   _____
   _____
   _____
   _____

   b. How they are different

   _____
   _____
   _____
   _____

3. INTENSITY—VOLUME
   a. How they are alike

   _____
   _____
   _____
   _____

   b. How they are different

   _____
   _____
   _____
   _____

4. LENS—MIRROR
   a. How they are alike

   _____
   _____
   _____
   _____

   b. How they are different

   _____
   _____
   _____
   _____

5. CONCAVE LENS—CONVEX LENS
   a. How they are alike

   _____
   _____
   _____
   _____

   b. How they are different

   _____
   _____
   _____
   _____

Sound and Light: Applying Ideas

Directions: Answer the following questions in the space provided.

1. Rank the following musical instruments according to the pitch of their sound. The highest pitch should be ranked as 1.

   _____ tuba   _____ flute   _____ trumpet

2. In the diagram, sonar is used to locate a sunken ship. If the sonar echo is heard after 3 seconds, how long did it take for the signal to reach the sunken ship? Why?

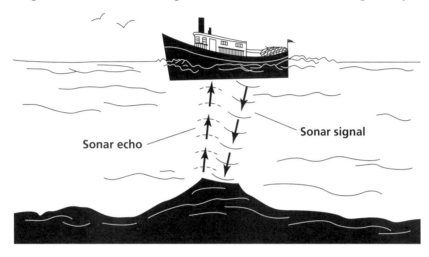

Sonar echo   Sonar signal

   _____

   _____

3. The range of human hearing is about 20–20,000 Hz. A dog can hear sounds in the range of 15–50,000 Hz. What can you conclude from this information? Circle the letter of the *best* answer.
   a. Dogs can hear sounds having a lower intensity than the sounds people hear.
   b. Dogs can hear sounds having a higher frequency than the sounds people hear.
   c. All sounds seem louder to dogs than to humans.

4. Astronomers use a unit of distance called a *light year* to measure distances between stars. A light year is the distance that light travels through space in one year. If sound could travel through empty space, would a "sound year" be a longer or shorter distance than a light year? Why?

   _____

   _____

5. How is a reflection in a mirror like an echo?

   _____

   _____

Word Search: Sound and Light

Directions: Write the correct word for each descriptive phrase. As a
check, find each vocabulary word in the puzzle below.

1. sound waves that humans cannot hear   _____

2. to move rapidly back and forth   _____

3. a form of energy that can be heard   _____

4. the unit used in measuring the intensity of a sound   _____

5. the number of vibrations per second   _____

6. one complete back-and-forth vibration   _____

7. how high or low a sound seems   _____

8. to bounce back sound or light waves   _____

9. a sound wave reflected back to its source   _____

10. a form of energy that can be seen   _____

Can you also find two terms that refer to the study of sound and the study of light? They are
acoustics and *optics*.

```
O  Q  F  J  B  X  K  V  N  F  P  H  G  F
V  T  U  Y  S  L  Z  E  L  F  N  W  R  R
X  V  L  C  Y  H  T  C  H  O  M  A  S  E
E  C  H  O  O  W  J  Y  O  F  T  C  O  Q
A  Y  Z  N  K  T  O  C  Y  Z  O  O  D  U
S  A  U  L  V  T  F  L  A  T  A  U  N  E
D  O  E  E  B  I  B  E  H  X  F  S  U  N
E  O  U  W  A  D  B  G  E  L  O  T  O  C
X  F  P  N  H  P  I  R  E  H  U  I  S  Y
M  T  B  T  D  L  I  B  A  O  Y  C  A  O
L  Y  C  B  I  O  I  T  C  T  C  S  R  Q
R  E  F  L  E  C  T  V  C  R  E  O  T  S
O  V  K  N  E  T  S  O  E  H  O  N  L  J
C  X  S  D  C  O  O  Y  B  W  K  F  U  S
```

Sound and Light: Terms Review

Part A

Directions: Match each term in Column A with its best description in Column B. Write the correct letter on the line.

Column A   **Column B**

_____ **1.** image

_____ **2.** decibel

_____ **3.** pitch

_____ **4.** frequency

_____ **5.** cycle

_____ **6.** convex mirror

_____ **7.** reflect

_____ **8.** concave mirror

a. How high or low a sound seems

b. One complete back-and-forth vibration

c. To bounce back sound or light waves

d. Likeness produced by reflected or refracted light waves

e. The number of vibrations per second

f. The unit used to measure the intensity of sound

g. Mirror that makes an enlarged imag

h. Mirror that makes a smaller image

Part B

Directions: Unscramble the word or words in parentheses to complete each sentence below.

9. _____ are particles of light.
           (topnosh)

10. An _____ is a sound wave reflected back to its source.
              (hoec)

11. A _____ is a flat mirror.
             (naple rimror)

12. The _____ is the band of colors that make up white light.
              (blisive crumpters)

Crossword: Electricity

Across

1. Force that keeps current flowing
4. Kind of circuit with an incomplete path for current
7. Device that breaks the circuit if the current gets too high
8. Unit used in measuring current
10. Unit of electric power
11. Type of circuit in which current flows along a single path
12. Type of current that changes direction regularly

Down

2. Material through which a current can pass easily
3. Energy from an electrical power source
4. Unit of resistance
5. A measure of how easily current will pass through a material
6. Type of diagram showing the parts of a circuit
9. Type of circuit in which current flows along more than one path

Compare and Contrast

Directions: When you compare and contrast things or ideas, you tell how they are alike and how they are different. Compare and contrast each pair below.

1. VOLT—AMPERE
   a. How they are alike

   _____
   _____
   _____

   b. How they are different

   _____
   _____
   _____
   _____

2. ALTERNATING CURRENT—DIRECT CURRENT
   a. How they are alike

   _____
   _____
   _____
   _____

   b. How they are different

   _____
   _____
   _____
   _____

3. DRY CELL BATTERY—WET CELL BATTERY
   a. How they are alike

   _____
   _____
   _____
   _____

   b. How they are different

   _____
   _____
   _____
   _____

4. CIRCUIT BREAKER—FUSE
   a. How they are alike

   _____
   _____
   _____
   _____

   b. How they are different

   _____
   _____
   _____
   _____

5. WATT—KILOWATT-HOUR
   a. How they are alike

   _____
   _____
   _____
   _____

   b. How they are different

   _____
   _____
   _____
   _____

Word Search: Electricity

Directions: Write the correct word for each definition. As a check,
find each vocabulary word in the puzzle below.

1. the movement of electrons from one place to another _____

2. the unit of electric power _____

3. the unit of electrical resistance _____

4. a measurement of how hard it is for current to flow
   through a material or circuit _____

5. a type of electricity that flows only in one direction (two words) _____

6. a type of electricity that continuously changes direction
   (two words) _____

7. a device that changes chemical energy into electrical energy _____

8. electrical energy from a power source _____

9. a type of circuit having more than one path for the current
   (two words) _____

10. a type of circuit having only one path for the current
    (two words) _____

```
P  B  C  C  S  D  V  I  V  U  K  R  O  U  B  M  E
H  P  D  A  E  S  F  D  B  A  T  T  E  R  Y  C  E
O  A  Z  D  R  Y  J  I  A  U  O  Y  E  P  N  A  O
C  R  U  M  I  C  I  R  C  E  L  M  Z  A  Z  D  R
K  A  T  I  E  U  C  E  X  R  V  C  T  O  H  M  D
O  L  A  S  S  R  M  C  L  F  M  S  I  T  K  O  U
E  L  Y  M  C  R  Z  T  C  X  I  L  R  O  A  V  W
K  E  W  W  I  E  D  C  E  S  U  J  K  S  M  R  D
E  L  E  S  R  N  W  U  E  Z  O  B  J  T  H  R  W
P  C  Z  V  C  T  T  R  T  T  A  W  O  R  L  E  R
C  I  N  R  U  Y  D  R  E  B  V  O  L  T  A  G  E
L  R  O  O  I  C  M  E  W  E  A  U  J  F  J  O  B
J  C  R  J  T  H  C  N  U  O  C  T  E  S  M  H  K
I  U  O  B  O  A  L  T  E  R  N  A  T  I  N  G  W
M  I  E  Y  E  B  X  W  S  W  B  R  X  E  O  K  X
N  T  C  O  R  C  U  R  R  E  N  T  P  J  R  X  O
```

Electricity: Terms Review

Part A
Directions: Match each term in Column A with its meaning in
Column B. Write the correct letter on the line.

Column A   **Column B**

_____ 1. conductor

_____ 2. direct current

_____ 3. series circuit

_____ 4. voltage

_____ 5. Ohm's law

_____ 6. resistance

_____ 7. parallel circuit

_____ 8. alternating current

a. The measurement of how hard it is for
electrons to flow through something

b. A type of circuit having more than one path
for the current

c. A type of electricity that continuously
changes direction

d. A material with very low resistance

e. A type of circuit having only one path for
the current

f. A type of electricity that flows in only one
direction

g. Energy from an electrical power source

h. Current equals voltage divided by resistance

Part B
Directions: Unscramble the word or words in parentheses to complete
each sentence below.

9. An _____ is a very poor conductor.
(salurtion)

10. The _____ of a battery are where electrons enter or leave.
(rainmelts)

11. A _____ is a device that changes chemical energy into electrical energy.
(treatby)

12. _____ is measured in volts.
(gavelot)

Math Connection: Using Ohm's Law

Directions: Use Ohm's law to answer the following questions. The
formula for Ohm's law is:

$$\text{current (amperes)} = \frac{\text{electromotive force (volts)}}{\text{resistance (ohms.}}$$

1. How much current does a headlight use with a 12-volt
   battery if it has a resistance of 3 ohms?   _____

2. How much current flows through a 100-ohm device
   connected to a 1.5-volt battery?   _____

3. What is the voltage of a 4-amp circuit with a
   resistance of 3 ohms?   _____

4. What is the resistance of a light bulb that uses
   0.5 amps and 110 volts?   _____

5. What is the resistance of an electric iron that takes
   12 amps at 120 volts?   _____

6. What is the current used by a toaster with a resistance
   of 12 ohms if it uses 120 volts?   _____

7. What is the voltage of a 2-amp circuit with a resistance
   of 0.75 ohms?   _____

8. What is the voltage of a battery that produces a 1.5-amp
   current through a resistance of 8 ohms?   _____

9. What happens to the current in a circuit as the
   voltage increases?   _____

10. What happens to the current in a circuit as the
    resistance increases?   _____

Crossword: Magnets

Across

1. Magnet made with an electric current

5. Device that works because of Earth's magnetism

8. Iron filings line up along a magnet's lines of _____ .

9. To push away

11. A magnetic _____ surrounds a magnet.

13. Not different

14. Device that attracts certain metals

Down

2. A natural magnet

3. To pull together

4. Instrument that uses magnets to make sound waves

6. Lines of force make up the _____ field.

7. Pole that attracts a north pole

10. There are two _____ on a magnet.

12. Opposite of *short*

Compare and Contrast

Directions: When you compare and contrast things or ideas, you tell
how they are alike and how they are different. Compare
and contrast each pair below.

1. NORTH POLE—SOUTH POLE
a. How they are alike

_____
_____
_____
_____

b. How they are different

_____
_____
_____
_____

2. HORSESHOE MAGNET—BAR MAGNET
a. How they are alike

_____
_____
_____

b. How they are different

_____
_____
_____
_____

3. ELECTROMAGNET—PERMANENT
MAGNET
a. How they are alike

_____
_____
_____
_____

b. How they are different

_____
_____
_____
_____

4. SPEAKER—MOTOR
a. How they are alike

_____
_____
_____
_____

b. How they are different

_____
_____
_____
_____

5. REPEL—ATTRACT
a. How they are alike

_____
_____
_____

b. How they are different

_____
_____
_____
_____

Word Search: Magnets

Directions: Write the correct word for each definition. As a check,
find each vocabulary word in the puzzle below.

1. a naturally magnetic stone _____

2. an object that will attract certain types of metals _____

3. area of lines of magnetic force (two words. _____

4. one of the two ends of a magnet; designated with N
(two words) _____

5. a device that becomes a magnet when electric current is
passed through a coil around it _____

6. to pull together _____

7. to push apart _____

8. a type of magnet shaped like a U (two words) _____

9. one of the two ends of a magnet; designated with S _____

10. to make into a magnet _____

```
Y  A  M  Y  A  F  F  W  K  T  C  E  G  J  K  V
F  J  M  A  O  I  S  O  U  T  H  P  O  L  E  C
T  H  M  M  G  M  L  W  D  P  A  P  M  E  K  K
R  O  M  L  A  N  F  C  R  J  U  L  L  X  C  A
I  R  N  C  E  G  E  W  A  S  N  O  Z  S  P  G
P  S  E  F  L  S  N  T  R  T  P  E  X  X  V  A
I  E  H  S  E  W  K  E  I  H  T  S  E  D  H  E
I  S  E  J  C  X  A  Y  T  C  P  R  M  G  S  N
W  H  B  W  T  T  O  R  J  I  F  O  A  A  L  E
J  O  C  Z  R  E  O  K  C  G  Z  I  I  C  N  G
J  E  G  Q  O  N  A  T  X  Q  E  E  E  O  T  B
I  M  W  X  M  R  E  P  E  L  M  S  T  L  J  X
U  A  U  U  A  N  K  I  C  M  G  S  W  A  D  X
O  G  D  B  G  E  C  E  U  M  E  M  T  I  U  O
M  N  E  A  N  I  Y  N  X  D  K  N  F  X  M  F
J  E  M  W  E  H  B  A  O  A  G  H  V  X  N  I
E  T  O  Z  T  F  F  L  C  L  Y  E  X  J  H  T
```

Magnets: Terms Review

Part A
Directions: Match each term in Column A with the best description in
Column B. Write the correct letter on the line.

Column A

_____ **1.** lodestone

_____ **2.** north pole

_____ **3.** mechanical energy

_____ **4.** electromagnet

_____ **5.** electromagnetism

_____ **6.** south pole

_____ **7.** magnetic field

_____ **8.** horseshoe magnet

Column B

a. Area of magnetism that surrounds a magnet

b. A magnet with a curved shape

c. One of the two ends of a magnet; designated by N

d. A naturally magnetic stone

e. What motors produce from electrical energy

f. A device that becomes a magnet when electric current passes through its coils

g. One of the two ends of a magnet; designated by S

h. The relationship between magnetism and electricity

Part B
Directions: Unscramble the word in parentheses to complete each
sentence below.

9. A _____ is a device that causes an electromagnet to turn.
(troom)

10. To _____ means to push apart.
(perle)

11. To _____ means to pull together.
(tarcatt)

12. A _____ is a device with a magnetic needle that always lines up with
(soapscm) Earth's magnetic field.